The Wrong Cat

by Narinder Dhami

illustrated by Alexandra Colombo

Meera and Mum were eating breakfast. Willow waited patiently for crumbs of buttered toast.

"Willow has an appointment at the vet," said Mum.

"Remember what happened last time, Mum?" Meera groaned. "Willow refused to get into her basket."

Willow hated going to the vet. She saw the basket and knew where she was going.

Meera and Mum took Willow's basket outside.
Willow couldn't work out what they were doing.

Meera put some treats inside the basket on the lawn. Suddenly, Willow understood! Willow was not going to be tricked. She was not going to get into the basket.

Then Willow saw another cat, walking in the bluebells. They had the same white patches and stripes on their legs. He could have been Willow's twin brother!

"Wait!" called Willow.

The other cat looked around.

"Wow! Am I looking in a mirror?" he gasped.

"I'm Willow and I live here," Willow said.

"I'm Stripe and I don't live anywhere," replied Stripe. "I'm a stray."

"So you never go to the vet?" asked Willow.

"I wouldn't mind that," Stripe sighed. "I just wish I had a human to care for me."

Suddenly, a sneaky plan popped into Willow's head.

"We could switch places," she said.

"I hate the vet and want to explore," Willow explained. "You want to be looked after, so it's perfect."

"Brilliant!" Stripe said, twitching his whiskers with delight.

Stripe crawled inside the basket and ate the treats. Soon, he had a full tummy. He happily dozed off.

Willow crawled under the hedge, out of sight.

"It worked! Willow's in the basket," Meera cried.

Quickly, Mum fastened the basket shut.

"Time to go to the vet," she whispered.

Willow watched Mum, Meera and Stripe drive off. She crawled out from under the hedge.

"Now I can explore!" Willow said excitedly.

Quickly, Willow climbed over the fence.

At last, Stripe woke up. A man was peering at him.

The vet had a confused expression on his face.

"There must be some mistake," he said. "This is a male cat!"

"So where is Willow?" Meera said in shock.

"Is this cat a stray?" Mum asked.

"Yes," nodded the vet. "I recognise him."

Meanwhile, Willow had enjoyed exploring. She'd met a ginger kitten and seen some very shiny fish. She started feeling hungry, so it was time to go home.

Willow wasn't certain of the way. Then she sniffed the air and her whiskers twitched. Home was *that* way!

When she got back, Meera and Stripe were playing with Willow's toy mouse.

"Willow!" Meera cried. "Where have you been?"

"Did you hate the vet?" Willow asked Stripe.

"No, he was very kind," said Stripe. "I'm going to live here now, Willow!"

"Great! I'll share my food and toys with you," Willow said.

"I'll go to the vet with you," said Stripe.

They both purred.

Cat Facts

- A male cat is called a Tom.
- A female cat is called a Queen.
- Cats have 230 bones while humans have just 206.
- Cats have 18 toes!

Encourage students to talk about the facts they have just read. Do they find any of them surprising?